Negotiating Exit Packages and Settlement Agreements

By Daniel Barnett

The Employment Law Library

All books in the Employment Law Library are sent for free to members of the HR Inner Circle.

1. Employee Investigations
2. GDPR for HR Professionals
3. Preventing and Defending Employee Stress Claims
4. Employment Tribunal Time Limits
5. Deconstructing TUPE
6. Changing Terms & Conditions
7. Constructive Dismissal
8. Resolving Grievances
9. HR Hazards
10. Employment Status
11. Spotting Malingering
12. Employment Tribunal Compensation
13. Hiring Staff
14. Computer and Social Media Misuse
15. Managing Sickness Absence
16. The Three Ps
17. Conflict at Work
18. SOSR Dismissals
19. Dismissing Problem Employees
20. Menopause and the Workplace
21. Dismissing Senior Executives
22. Negotiating Exit Packages and Settlement Agreements

Published by HR Inner Circle Limited, Unit 3, Chequers Farm, Chequers Lane, Watford, Hertfordshire WD25 0LG

ISBN 978-1-918091-01-4

Acknowledgments

Welcome to book 22 in this series of mini-guides on employment law for HR Professionals. It accompanies an online course on settlement agreements, which should be available from www.danielbarnett.com from summer 2025.

Thanks to Francesca Read and Jackie Le Poidevin for their help with the first draft of this book.

Thanks also to Tincuta Collett for the layout and design, Aaron Gaff for proofreading and Maria Rodriguez for converting the book into the formats needed for Amazon.

None of these books are possible without the input and experience of the members of the HR Inner Circle. I write these small books for you, and you get them for free as part of your membership.

If you're not a member of the HR Inner Circle and you're interested in learning more about membership (www.hrinnercircle.co.uk), there is some information at the back of this book.

Daniel Barnett
December 2025

About the Author

Daniel Barnett is a leading employment law barrister practising from Outer Temple Chambers. With 25 years' experience defending public and private sector employers against employment claims, he has represented a Royal Family, several international airlines, FTSE-100 companies and various NHS Trusts and local authorities. Employee clients include David & Victoria Beckham's nanny and Paul Mason (subject of the ITV documentary 'Britain's Fattest Man').

Daniel is a past chair of the Employment Lawyers' Association's publishing committee and electronic services working party. He is the author or co-author of eight books, including the Law Society Handbook on Employment Law (currently in its 8th edition). He is the creator of the Employment Law (UK) mailing list, an email alerter bulletin service sending details of breaking news in employment law three times a week to 33,000 recipients.

Legal directories describe him as 'extremely knowledgeable and [he] can absorb pages of instructions at lightning speed', 'involved in a number of highly contentious matters', 'singled out for his work for large blue-chip companies', 'combination of in-depth legal knowledge, pragmatism, quick response times and approachability', 'inexhaustible', 'tenacious', 'knowledgeable', and 'an excellent advocate'.

He is one of the leading speakers and trainers on the employment law and HR circuit. He has presented seminars for the House of Commons, the BBC, Oxford University, HSBC, Barclays Bank, Ocado, and dozens of other organisations in-house. In 2013, 2014, 2016, and 2019 he designed — and was the sole speaker at — the Employment Law MasterClass national tour.

As well as full-time practice as a barrister and speaker, Daniel is the founder of the HR Inner Circle – a membership club for smart, ambitious HR Professionals. In 2007, he co-founded CPD Webinars Ltd, then the UK's leading webinar training company for lawyers, and sold it to Thomson Reuters in 2011. Daniel is widely sought after as a commentator in both broadcast and print media on all legal issues. Since 2010 he has presented the Legal Hour on LBC Radio. In 2019, he launched Employment Law Matters, a weekly podcast with short explanations of employment law topics. Subscribe at www.danielbarnett.co.uk/podcast

www.danielbarnett.co.uk
Temple, London

DANIEL BARNETT
BARRISTER
SUBSCRIBE
HOME
COMMUNITY
CHANNELS
ABOUT
HELP I'M BEING BULLIED AT WORK
Help - I'm being bullied at work: a practical guide for...
Daniel Barnett
4.5K views • 3 weeks ago
The most heartbreaking, emotional call I've ever take...
Daniel Barnett
1.2K views • 3 weeks ago
HOW TO HANDLE DISCIPLINARY DISMISSAL AND PERFORMANCE MANAGEMENT
How to Handle Disciplinary, Dismissal and Performance...
Daniel Barnett
688 views • 1 month ago
ASK THE PRESIDENT
EMPLOYMENT TRIBUNALS PRESIDENT (E&W) JUDGE BARRY CLARKE
FAIRNESS IN REDUNDANCY SELECTION
REBECCA TUCK QC
Fair Redundancy Dismissals with Rebecca Tuck QC
Daniel Barnett
1K views • 2 weeks ago
Help - I'm being bullied at work: a practical guide for...
Daniel Barnett
4.5K views • 3 weeks ago
CHANGING TERMS AND CONDITIONS AFTER A TUPE TRANSFER
THE UK'S LEADING YOUTUBE CHANNEL FOR LAW EXPLAINER VIDEOS
WWW.YOUTUBELEGAL.CO.UK

Contents

1. When to consider settling 11

2. How to assess the claim's strength 19

3. The cost of not settling 25

4. Understand the tax treatment of settlement sums 29

5. How to open negotiations when a dispute has already arisen 33

6. How to get the ball rolling in other situations 39

7. Making an Offer 45

8. Seven secret weapons: things you can give that the employee will want 49

9. Common employee strategies and how to respond 53

10. Employer strategies: how to keep the pressure on 59

11. Top tips from the experts: books on negotiation 65

12. Putting negotiation theory into practice 71

13. How to create a legally binding settlement agreement 75

14. Settlement agreements: practical pointers 81

15. Ten settlement agreement clauses to protect yourself 87

16. The aftermath of the negotiations 93

Chapter 1

When to consider settling

As anyone working in HR knows, the relationship between employer and employee does not always run smoothly. Employers can often tackle issues using traditional tools like the disciplinary or performance processes. But for many different reasons, employers sometimes do not want to follow a lengthy process. Instead, they want to quickly reach a formal, legally binding settlement with an employee. This usually involves the employee exiting the business (if they haven't already done so).

This first chapter focuses on what settlement is all about, when a business might want to consider settling and when it might not.

What does 'settlement' mean?

A settlement, according to the Oxford English Dictionary, is 'an official agreement that ends an argument'. In the employment world, when a business 'settles' with an employee, it reaches an agreement with them that generally provides a clean break – the past stays in the past and, crucially, cannot be the subject of legal action by the employee. Chapter 13 of this book covers what such an agreement needs to look like and the legal requirements it needs to meet to be binding.

Points to consider when weighing up whether to settle

From an employer's perspective, settling is about power and control of the process and risk. There are key questions to ask yourself when considering whether to suggest a settlement or not.

Key questions to help you decide if settling is the best strategy

What are the risks involved in not settling?

How unconstrained can you be in your negotiations – how much money do you have to play with, and do you think it will be enough to 'seal the deal'?

How much appetite does the business have to fight a claim, regardless of its merits?

What's the employee's position? Are they in a dodgy financial position? Will their money troubles make them open to a deal? Do you think they have the appetite to bring a claim?

What kind of message could a settlement send to other staff?

You'll learn about assessing risk in Chapters 2 and 3. You must weigh the risk of losing litigation (and the certainty of lost management time and irrecoverable costs) against paying money to someone you may feel is undeserving. You'll be paying to bring closure and confidentiality to the issue at stake.

Situations when you might decide to settle

Fighting a claim, even if you have right on your side, usually takes up a lot of time, costs a significant amount of money and can be extremely distracting. A recent study by David Millner, the HR Curator, showed that a business spent £340,000 on legal fees and management time to defend a discrimination claim – that it still lost. And the employee had been willing to settle for £45,000.

Apart from saving time, money and effort, these are other reasons you may have for settling.

To reward the employee

You may want to treat an employee generously to reward them and show other staff that loyal service reaps benefits even if they have to leave. This only works if the employee's departure is not their fault, as otherwise, you could be seen to be rewarding bad behaviour or poor performance.

This is a reaction we often see when senior executives receive large termination payments. Look at Liz Truss, who was given a payout of almost £20,000 after resigning from her very short tenure as Prime Minister. Or Google, which a few years ago reportedly gave one of its top executives a $90 million payoff, despite sexual misconduct claims.

To maintain goodwill

The employee may have influence in your industry, so their opinion of how they have been treated needs to be kept positive.

To smooth the sale of the business

If you are selling your business, the purchaser may want all claims sorted out before the sale. This avoids the need for you, as the seller, to put aside large amounts of money in case of future claims, which the sale document will usually make you liable for.

To buy silence

You may need to keep the employee quiet because they have potentially embarrassing or damaging information. Post Weinstein and the #MeToo movement, settlement agreements cannot contain absolute gagging clauses – this is covered in Chapter 13 – and you can't sweep illegality under the carpet. But there will be times when it may be better to appease a disgruntled employee so you can avoid revelations that would cause disruption.

Situations when you may decide not to settle

Sometimes, settling is not advisable due to the other risks.

Looking guilty

Some allegations may be too damaging for you to be seen to settle them. What was your reaction when Prince Andrew reportedly paid £12 million to someone who accused him of sexual impropriety? Sometimes, a settlement might look like an admission of guilt. This is also a risk when there have been whistleblowing allegations, or you are in a heavily regulated industry, such as pharmaceuticals or financial services.

Colleagues seeing the recipient as undeserving

People might see the employee as undeserving of the settlement. This could be because they have harassed someone or been dishonest or disruptive. You should not underestimate how easy it is to lose employees' respect by paying money to someone whose dismissal they regard as deserved.

Copycat claims

People might see you as an easy target if you offer settlements too easily. Even if the details stay secret, word spreads. Settling, even for a small sum, might backfire because confidentiality provisions in the agreement mean you cannot let staff know you only settled for a nominal amount.

Other considerations

These are other points that may affect your decision to settle.

Employee insurance

Employees sometimes have legal expenses insurance, perhaps as an add-on with their house and car insurance. If they do, they may be slower to settle. But it doesn't make settlement impossible by any means.

Legal insurers assess claims through a 'merits' process, which involves a valuation of the claim. If the employee refuses an offer within the valuation window, they will often lose their insurance cover. In these cases, if you want to settle, set out the claim's weaknesses in writing early on. This document will find its way in front of the insurers. They, like you, are undertaking a risk management process here, so it's best to appear happy to fight the claim and have a robust defence ready. This could tip the balance towards a settlement.

Employer insurance

Some businesses have insurance that provides cover for legal representation if a claim arises. Some products also cover compensation if you lose.

If you have insurance cover, this may tip the balance against settling, as you have protection against litigation costs. But insurance only takes away some of the pain of tribunal proceedings. You still have to factor in business disruption, potential reputational damage and possible compensation. Also, the insurer can settle without your permission if it thinks this is financially sensible. Make sure you consult with your insurer closely throughout, as taking any steps in litigation (or making a settlement offer) without their agreement might invalidate the insurance cover.

An element of unfairness

Sometimes, despite being seen as merited, an element of the dismissal may be unfair, exposing you to risk.

In this case, you will often want to refuse to settle at first but keep the matter under review. Claims usually take a long time to come to tribunal, and the longer things drag on, the more likely the employee is to run out of funds or energy. Also, settling a year or so after the dismissal will probably damage staff morale less than doing so shortly after it.

If dismissal is justified (despite making some mistakes with the procedure), if the claim does go to tribunal, its financial worth to the employee is likely to be less than they hope. Chapter 3 focuses on how to assess a claim's worth.

Problems with witnesses

It's often easier to fight a claim if the witnesses all still work for you. If a key witness has left, is leaving or is no longer friendly to the business, you may not be able to put your 'best foot forward' when mounting your defence.

An immovable employee

Most settlements are fairly easy to agree because both sides want closure and to move on. But sometimes, an employee becomes entrenched and 'wants justice' or wants to make a point or extract more money from you than you are willing or able to pay.

In these circumstances, you may decide not to settle and back away from the negotiating table. The ball is then in the employee's court, and they need to decide whether to go ahead with legal proceedings against you.

Remember, the door is never closed on settlement. Many claims get all the way to the door of the tribunal – at which point that 'derisory' offer you made several months previously suddenly looks attractive to the litigating employee.

Chapter 2

How to assess the claim's strength

To assess the employee's chance of winning the claim, you need to look at three things.

1. What exactly is being alleged

Sometimes, an employee won't clearly articulate what their grievance is. It's entirely legitimate for you to ask them to explain it properly. They may not be able to explain it in legal terms, but they need to be able to say what the perceived wrongdoing on their employer's part is and how they have suffered as a result.

2. What the law says about that type of allegation

Next, you need to assess the allegation in terms of the law. To do this, ask yourself:

- Is (or was) the individual an employee, worker or independent contractor? Their rights will depend on their status. Determining someone's employment status can be complex and nuanced, so you may need professional help to do this. You could also look at my book on Employment Status, available as a free download for members of www.hrinnercircle.co.uk.

- If the individual was an employee and has been dismissed, were they with you long enough to claim unfair dismissal? Unless the dismissal was for an automatically unfair reason, they currently need two years' continuous employment to be eligible. Note that the government intends to allow employees to claim unfair dismissal from Day One in the job, although it will be easier to dismiss during an initial period of employment. (At the time of writing, early 2025, the government is indicating that will be the first nine months of employment.) The earliest this reform will take effect is Autumn 2026.
- Could an element of the dismissal result in an automatically unfair dismissal claim? This could relate to trade union activities by the employee, whistleblowing, health and safety issues or other aspects, some of which are quite rare.
- If the employee resigned and is claiming constructive dismissal, the legal test they have to pass is that they resigned in response to a fundamental breach of contract by their employer. So, how serious was the breach they are complaining about? Did they resign in response to it or were other reasons at play?
- Is there an element of discrimination involved? Don't just think about direct discrimination, which is fairly rare, or harassment. Think about indirect discrimination, victimisation and discrimination

arising from a disability. Think also about less obvious situations, such as whether someone's performance or conduct may have been affected by, for example, being neurodivergent or experiencing menopause symptoms.

- Is there a breach of contract claim? How much may that be worth?

3. What happened

To assess the strength of the threatened claim, you need to know exactly what happened. This can be tricky, especially if you've been too close to the situation. Getting a fresh pair of eyes to look at the matter can be helpful, such as someone you trust from outside your organisation. If nobody comes to mind, you can approach an independent HR Professional or a lawyer for an opinion.

Example

An employee, Lee, resigns. He says he has been forced to do so because his manager has been bullying him, and he claims constructive dismissal. Lee has been with the company for 15 years and until recently has been a reliable and respected employee.

You know the manager has been performance managing Lee for the past six months because he became careless in his work output, started taking risks, became easily distracted and argumentative, was frequently late and took a lot of time off sick. The manager took Lee carefully through the company's performance improvement process, monitoring him regularly and giving him targets and progressive warnings. Lee resigned immediately after receiving a final written warning.

Lee's solicitors have just written to say that Lee suffers from bipolar disorder and his performance issues arose directly from that condition, which deteriorated when his medication was changed. They say the company should have considered this in performance managing him and they are now threatening a disability discrimination claim.

To assess the risk of a successful claim, you should find answers to these questions:

What type of disability discrimination is Lee alleging? Direct? Failure to make reasonable adjustments, and if so, which adjustments? Discrimination arising from a disability? Ask his solicitors to spell out exactly what is being alleged, but don't put ideas into their heads.

- What exactly did the company know about Lee's bipolar condition?
- If the company did know about it, what adjustments did it make? Was it reasonable not to make the adjustments that Lee alleges should have been made?
- If the company didn't know about the bipolar disorder, should the sudden and uncharacteristic change in Lee's performance have alerted it?

- What explanations did Lee give for his drop in performance before resigning?
- Was the final written warning issued in accordance with the performance improvement plan (PIP)?

If there was no knowledge of the condition within the company, Lee didn't mention it when asked about his change in performance and the PIP was followed scrupulously, you will probably decide that the chance of the claims succeeding is slim.

However, a tribunal could decide that the sudden marked change would have alerted a reasonable employer to a possible medical issue, so the company should have sent Lee for a medical examination before embarking on the PIP to establish whether reasonable adjustments were required. If they were, Lee could have a successful disability discrimination claim. Issuing a final written warning without exploring disability or making reasonable adjustments could amount to a fundamental breach of trust and confidence, meaning the constructive dismissal claim could succeed too.

To assess the risks accurately, you need a good understanding of employment law and the facts of the case. Where a claim's merits are debatable or finely balanced, you can take a strong stance in the settlement negotiations and work to sow doubt in the employee's mind. Here, you might suggest to Lee that he failed to tell you about his bipolar condition, there was no way you could have guessed he was disabled and the process you followed was watertight. You might also explain how hard it is to win constructive unfair dismissal claims.

A wise or well-advised employee will not want to risk significant costs pursuing a claim with uncertain prospects when they can walk away immediately with a reasonable sum in settlement.

Chapter 3
The cost of not settling

You need to think about the costs of not settling. These are four aspects to consider.

1. What the employee could reasonably win

Some claims are easier to quantify than others, so it is only possible to provide general advice on what the claim might cost you. If you want to learn more about how to calculate potential compensation, another book in this series, *Employment Tribunal Compensation*, explains in detail exactly how a tribunal will work out the amount you'll be ordered to pay to a successful claimant.

However, here are the key amounts the employee may be entitled to if their claim is successful. (Note that the figures given are correct as of April 2024 – the statutory amounts change every year in April.)

Elements of a compensation payment

Notice pay

This is whatever is payable under the employment contract. Notice pay is taxable. Regardless of what the contract says, the employee will be entitled to statutory minimum notice at the very least. This is one week for each year of service, up to a maximum of 12 weeks after 12 years.

Holiday pay

This will be whatever holiday is accrued but untaken at the point of dismissal. This payment is also taxable.

Basic award

The employee will be eligible for this payment if they are claiming unfair dismissal or there's a redundancy situation. The award is calculated in the same way as statutory redundancy pay, so employees get a multiple of a week's gross pay (capped at £719 per week), with the multiple set out in a statutory formula. You can use the 'ready reckoner' at gov.uk to do the calculations for you.

Unfair dismissal compensatory award

This compensates the employee for lost earnings due to their dismissal. This element is capped at 52 weeks' gross pay or £118,223, whichever is lower. If the employee establishes discrimination or whistleblowing, this cap will not apply.

Injury to feelings award

This is available in discrimination cases. It's a punitive award that is technically unlimited, but tribunals generally use three different bands (known as the 'Vento bands'), depending on the severity of the discrimination. These are currently set at:

- **One-off act of discrimination:** £1,200-£12,100
- **Serious discrimination but not long-term (this includes dismissal):** £12,100-£36,400
- **Ongoing discrimination taking place over several years:** £36,400-£60,700

Many arguments are available that you can deploy during your negotiations with the employee to reduce the settlement amount. These are covered in Chapters 8 and 10.

2. Legal fees

You should start by checking whether the business has any form of insurance that covers employment claims. If it does, check the terms.

Does the insurance cover legal representation in the tribunal? Usually, it does, but you must follow the insurer's advice and normally use the insurer's panel solicitors. Does it cover any award that a tribunal might make? If it does, bear in mind the insurer won't cover any contractual claims, such as notice pay, unpaid wages or holiday pay. Is there any excess? Are any claims not covered? It's important to read the small print at an early stage – the last thing you want is to unwittingly do something that invalidates your cover.

If insurance is not in place, you need to be aware that (in almost all cases) each side bears its own legal costs when bringing and defending tribunal proceedings. You must go into negotiations with your eyes open and understand that the business is unlikely to get back any of the money it ploughs into defending a claim. This is lost money – and a pot that you could potentially bring to the table as part of a settlement package.

To give you an idea of legal fees, a law firm based in the South East quotes an indicative cost of £14,000-£17,000 to defend a straightforward unfair dismissal claim. Another firm quotes up to £30,000 for defending complex cases. If you're taking legal advice and using a barrister, then legal costs can increase very quickly indeed.

3. Lost time

Preparing the company's defence will take up management time. Preparing witness statements and managing documentary disclosure all take time. Also, if the case goes to hearing, witnesses will need to take time out of the business to give evidence. All this is a distraction to the business, causing anxiety for staff and lost opportunity costs for the company. Standing firm and fighting on principle is not always a good decision.

4. Staff welfare

It's important to consider early on who your likely witnesses will be. Are any of them vulnerable members of staff? Are you concerned for their welfare should they need to give evidence? An indirect cost in the form of staff illness or absence because of their involvement in any legal claim may tip the balance towards settlement.

Chapter 4

Understand the tax treatment of settlement sums

How tax works in relation to settlement sums is a key factor when preparing to come to the negotiating table. You need to look at not only what you will offer your employee but also what they will get in their pocket once tax is taken into account. After all, it is that sum the employee will be focused on!

Although tax can be very complex, it's important to get the calculations right. This is because HMRC will usually pursue the employer for unpaid tax and employee National Insurance contributions (NICs) – and will always pursue it for unpaid employer's NICs, of course.

You should get tax advice if the settlement agreement is unusual, but these are some simple principles to bear in mind:

- Any payments made up to the termination date will be taxable unless they relate to discrimination. You must therefore always be clear in the settlement agreement what the termination date is.

- Any post-termination payment of the employee's basic pay for any period of unserved notice is subject to tax and class 1 NICs.

- A payment for entering into a restrictive covenant is taxable.

- A termination payment is exempt from tax up to a £30,000 threshold if it is made in connection with the termination of employment and is not post-termination notice pay. This includes payments made to non-executive directors.

- You must add together all eligible payments when working out whether you have reached the £30,000 threshold, including payments made over several tax years and in relation to different jobs with the same employer. Any termination payment above the threshold is subject to tax and employer's NICs.

- Most contractual payments are taxable. The exception is contractual redundancy payments, which are tax free up to the £30,000 threshold.

- Payments into a registered pension that are made in connection with the termination of employment are tax free. They do not count towards the £30,000 ceiling.

The tax-free threshold of £30,000 can form a helpful focus in certain cases, although its importance depends a lot on the overall potential claim value. If you are near or over the ceiling, you can look to structure the payments to work around this, as the following example illustrates.

Example

It is March 2025. Joe works as an accounts director. He is 41 years old and has 10 years' service. He is in dispute with his employer because he feels he is being bullied. He has raised a grievance, and his employer has entered into negotiations with him with a view to ending his employment under a settlement agreement.

Joe's notice pay is £10,000. The business has offered him an additional £40,000 in full and final settlement of his claims. Joe will only accept if he can pay little or no tax on the payment. He intends to take a career break once he leaves the business while he decides what to do next.

Joe can get up to £30,000 tax free as compensation for loss of employment. It is only any amount above this that is vulnerable to tax: £10,000 in Joe's case. So, what can you do to reduce the tax payable by Joe on this amount so you can get the deal over the line?

Options include:

- Offering to divert some of the £40,000 into Joe's pension, where it will not be subject to income tax or NICs.
- Splitting the payment and paying any amount over £30,000 after 5 April. It will then be subject to tax in the following tax year. If Joe's career break means that he earns nothing or very little in that tax year, then he may pay little or no tax on this extra sum.

Remember, you must pay tax at source on Joe's notice pay of £10,000. This is non-negotiable. It is a contractual payment.

Chapter 5
How to open negotiations when a dispute has already arisen

This chapter and Chapter 6 will take you through the different ways in which a settlement negotiation with an employee can begin. From a legal point of view, the dos and don'ts vary depending on the situation. This chapter focuses on the correct process to follow when there's an active dispute between the parties.

How do you know if there's a dispute and why is this important?

You must consider carefully whether the business is in 'dispute' with the employee. You can only hold discussions on a 'without prejudice' basis – which means that what is said or written can't be disclosed or used in tribunal – if there's a 'dispute'. Discussing a settlement with an employee is risky; you want to be able to speak freely and put your cards on the table, but you don't want what you've said to be used against you in any future claim.

You can only rely on the without prejudice rule if the following elements exist:

1. There is a dispute.

2. You have made an offer.

3. That offer is a genuine attempt to settle the dispute.

Elements two and three are straightforward – the business wants to make an offer and wants to reach a settlement. The tricky bit is the first element – whether a dispute has yet arisen in a legal sense.

If, for example, you want to dismiss an employee and this is the first conversation about the dismissal, it would be difficult to argue that the conversation is a genuine attempt to settle an existing dispute – because there is currently no dispute. There might well be a dispute by the time the conversation ends, but there won't be one at the start of the conversation, so the start of the conversation won't be off the record and without prejudice.

How bad do things have to be for there to be a 'dispute'? It doesn't have to be 'handbags at dawn' but there does have to be a difference of opinion and a lack of agreement. The case of *BNP Paribas v Mezzotero UKEAT/0218/04* held that the act of raising a grievance, on its own, does not mean there is a dispute between employee and employer in a 'without prejudice' sense. A grievance is the raising of a concern. It is not a dispute, although it may become one if the employee disagrees with the employer's response. There is usually a tipping point in these situations.

If you intend a meeting to be 'without prejudice', you should say so at the outset. If a meeting starts without dispute but a dispute develops, then you should be ready to pause and confirm that the rest of the meeting will be without prejudice.

A pragmatic approach is best – use the language of 'without prejudice' freely and often. It cannot do any harm! But be aware that you might not, if push comes to shove, be able to rely on a discussion having been without prejudice if you had it before a dispute arose.

How to get the ball rolling

At the start of any meeting with the employee, you should say that it is being held on a 'without prejudice and subject to contract' basis. It's also good practice to explain what this means. Most people don't understand the term in the legal sense – it isn't exactly an 'off-the-record' conversation.

Explain that:

- **Without prejudice** exchanges allow you and the employee to speak freely. Whatever is said cannot be used against each other in proceedings if no settlement occurs.
- **Subject to contract** means that only the final written and signed settlement agreement is binding. Nothing agreed verbally is binding until it's signed.

It's important to invest time in this initial conversation as it sets the scene and gives you an opportunity to explain the company's perspective before the employee goes to see their lawyer or union representative. You might like to use a script to help you.

If you're putting anything relating to the settlement of a dispute in writing, then write 'without prejudice and subject to contract' at the top of the letter. This means any offer made in the correspondence will be off the record and subject to the employee agreeing the terms of a wider agreement that will set out the settlement terms in full. This allows you to make a 'headline' offer without having to pull together a full draft settlement agreement (which can be a little overwhelming for an employee). You will be safe in the knowledge that this letter, on its own, can't bind you.

When writing to the employee or their representative, always think about whether to mark the communication as 'without prejudice' or whether you would be happy for a tribunal to view it (referred to as 'open' or 'on-the-record' correspondence). It's not advisable to mix without prejudice and open correspondence in the same letter or email.

Example

To illustrate how not to write to an employee setting out a proposed settlement, let's look at this letter. See if you can spot the issues.

> Dear Mr Miller
>
> **'Off the record' – attendance management meeting and offer of settlement**
>
> During our off-the-record discussion on Thursday, we discussed your current levels of attendance, and, because of that discussion, we invite you to a Stage 3 attendance hearing on Monday 16 June at 12.30pm. We have attached all relevant documents. You are entitled to be accompanied at this meeting by a work colleague or trade union representative. Please note that one possible outcome could be the termination of your employment.

> We separately made an off-the-record offer to you to end your employment with us. If you want to accept our offer of £3,000 in full and final settlement of any employment claims, please sign where indicated below and return the letter to us.
>
> If you sign this letter, your termination date will be Monday 16 June, and you won't need to come to the meeting we mentioned above.
>
> Yours sincerely

Four key mistakes have been made here:

1. The use of the phrase 'off the record'. This is an everyday phrase that most people understand, but it is not the right one to use when you are offering a settlement to an employee. The words 'without prejudice' should be used when there's already a dispute.

2. The employer has made an offer in the second paragraph, but it doesn't state that this is 'subject to contract'. This wording is important as, if the employee is interested, it will allow the employer to follow up with a full settlement agreement.

3. The letter suggests that the settlement can be completed merely by the employee counter-signing the letter. Chapter 13 will explore this in more detail, but just signing the letter would not legally settle any employment claims the employee might have. A formal settlement agreement or Acas COT3 agreement is needed to do this. So, the employer might be throwing

£3,000 at the employee without in any way reducing the risk of litigation – a very bad idea.

4. The letter mixes open and without prejudice correspondence. The whole letter is headed 'off the record' but the first paragraph is an attempt to move forward an open attendance management process. The employer should keep this process entirely separate from the without prejudice offer. It should send two separate letters.

Chapter 6
How to get the ball rolling in other situations

This chapter explores the first steps you should take towards negotiating an exit when you are not in a 'dispute' with the employee, as well as what to do if it's the employee who approaches you asking for a settlement. It also covers some tips for the correct language to protect the business's position during the negotiation process and before you reach a binding agreement.

How to open the conversation when there's no dispute

If you want to talk to an employee about exiting the organisation but there is no dispute between you, the without prejudice rule does not apply. So, any conversation about settling is at risk of being disclosed. Even worse, the employee could later say this was unreasonable conduct on your part, giving rise to potential claims.

It's more common than you might realise for a business to consider exiting an employee by cutting to the chase and offering them a settlement. Quite often, issues with employees are allowed to fester. They are not handled openly until one day, the employee's manager explodes and says, 'That's it! They've got to go!' However, the employee has no idea there's a problem and, more crucially, no fair, open performance management process has been followed.

This is where 'pre-termination discussions' come in. These are permitted under section 111A of the *Employment Rights Act 1996* (ERA 1996) and allow you to make a settlement offer to an employee before dismissal and before any dispute arises. The fact that the conversation has taken place and details of what was said can't be used in any later unfair dismissal proceedings unless you acted improperly.

Pre-termination discussions, also known as 'protected conversations', are a poor substitute for without prejudice negotiations. They only protect discussions from disclosure for most types of unfair dismissal claims. If the employee alleges discrimination or any other employment law breach, then the facts and content of the discussion are disclosable.

It is therefore recommended that, even if you start with a pre-termination discussion (because there's no dispute), you also use the language of 'without prejudice'. In reality, once you have held that first meeting with the employee to put your cards on the table, you're likely to be in a 'dispute' anyway, so it's a good idea to refer to both systems.

It's sensible to have a script prepared ahead of your meeting. Tell the employee at the start of the meeting that you want to have a pre-termination discussion with them and explain what this means. Given the risk that your discussions may be disclosable in any claim except for ordinary unfair dismissal, you must be very careful what you say, as the example below illustrates. You can always give further details later, when you have the dispute needed to engage the without prejudice rule.

Example

Joan is a tailor. She has refused to carry out an instruction to use her sewing machine in a certain way. Her boss thinks Joan is annoying and wants to make her an offer to leave the business.

So, is there a dispute here? Probably not. At most, you have a petty frustration. This means any conversation about the settlement will need to be raised as a pre-termination discussion in the first instance.

Her boss meets with Joan and says at the beginning that it is a pre-termination discussion. When he mentions the sewing machine instruction, Joan explains she had raised concerns that the employer's method was dangerous. Her boss says he finds her annoying and offers her a settlement agreement. Joan refuses and resigns, claiming automatic unfair dismissal on whistleblowing grounds.

Will this conversation be disclosable? It wouldn't have been for an ordinary unfair dismissal claim. However, Joan is claiming she blew the whistle on poor health and safety, which is one of the exceptions to the 'protected conversation' rule, so the discussion will be disclosable.

This illustrates the importance of treading very carefully when you approach an employee with a settlement offer. Be on alert for anything they say that might take the situation outside the ordinary unfair dismissal realm.

What if the employee comes to the table first?

It's normally the employer that approaches the employee to make a settlement offer. Sometimes, though, the employee comes to the table first and actively asks for a settlement. Usually, this is because a formal process is already underway, and they can see the 'writing on the wall' and want to jump before they are pushed.

The same principles regarding without prejudice and pre-termination discussions apply here. However, you can take some comfort from the employee coming to you first, as they are unlikely to take issue with settlement discussions they themselves have initiated.

A few things you might want to consider if the employee comes to you include:

- Whether you actually want the employee to leave. If you don't, discuss what has prompted them to approach you and see if you can resolve any issues.
- Any offer you might make, bearing in mind you are likely to be in a better bargaining position if the employee has approached you. Think what the business might be able to get out of the settlement – this is discussed in Chapter 15.
- Whether it's appropriate to settle at all. If the employee is asking for serious allegations against them to be dropped, settling may send the wrong message.

Internal and external communications: protect your position

As you now know, written correspondence sent to an employee about a settlement should be marked 'without prejudice and subject to contract'. In the case of a pre-termination discussion, your written communications to the employee should also state that the discussion is covered by section 111A of the ERA 1996 and explain what this means.

But what about discussions that might be going on behind the scenes with other people about the situation? You might take some legal advice about the situation and assume your lawyers will never have to disclose this advice if discussions break down and the employee brings a claim. This is not necessarily true, and you need to be careful.

There is something called 'legal advice privilege' that protects advice given by a lawyer from disclosure. However, it is not without limit. Importantly, it only applies to advice given to a 'client', meaning a person or group of people authorised to instruct a lawyer. This is quite a narrow definition. If one of your managers starts sending copies of advice received far and wide, it may lose its protection. It is advisable to have a clearly defined 'client team' – don't let legal advice or documents seep any wider than this.

Also, importantly, 'legal advice privilege' only covers discussions you have with your lawyers. It does not cover communications you have with external/independent HR Professionals, so be careful what you put in writing. Once litigation is likely and the dominant purpose of the communications is defending that litigation, something called ‘litigation privilege’ arises, which protects communications with external HR Professionals. But until then, be careful.

If you prepare documents for your solicitor, make sure you send them over. Otherwise, they will not be covered by legal advice privilege and are disclosable.

Avoid regurgitating legal advice you’ve received in other forms. If you copy and paste advice or paraphrase it and send it out to others internally, it will lose privilege. The original document from the lawyer would have attracted privilege but your cut-and-paste job will not.

Finally, documents sent between managers, or between managers and HR, are not covered by legal advice privilege. That’s important. They are disclosable in litigation unless they have been prepared for the dominant purpose of litigation (which, pre-dismissal, will be hard to establish). So, be careful about what you write in emails or WhatsApp messages. Remind managers to ‘keep their powder dry’ and avoid airing their views openly in internal correspondence.

Chapter 7
Making an Offer

Chapters 2 and 3 explored how to analyse the financial risk posed by an employee you are considering settling with and how to work out the worst-case scenario if discussions break down. By following this process, you can also hopefully come up with some areas of weakness in the employee's position that you can use, if necessary, during your negotiations.

This preparation gives you the parameters within which the business is comfortable to negotiate. How much, though, should you actually offer the employee as a starting point? This chapter focuses on how to get to your opening figure.

Avoiding confusion

The first point to make is that it's important to keep track of exactly what offer is on the table at any given time – what has been accepted and what has been rejected. If you don't do this, you risk a situation where the employee thinks you have reached settlement A and you think you have reached settlement B. You draw up the paperwork and then realise you've agreed something different to the employee. This wastes time and causes negotiations to lose momentum or even collapse because each side thinks the other is acting in bad faith.

To avoid this, make sure you:

- Always set out any offer **in writing**. Follow up a verbal offer with written confirmation. It's harder to get confused if something is written in black and white.
- State that all verbal or written offers are '**without prejudice and subject to contract**'. Offers generally deal with headline terms only – basically, the money side of things. But it must be clear you will require the employee to sign a full settlement agreement in return for the monetary offer.

Your opening gambit: how low can you go?

Obviously, you're not going to go in with your best offer straight away and leave yourself nowhere to go in the negotiations if the employee turns you down. Likewise, you generally don't want to pitch an opening offer so low that it's insulting and escalates the tension. But sometimes, you do want to 'lowball' so the employee comes back with a counter-offer and you know what the upper parameter of settlement is.

Here are three tips to help you decide on your opening offer:

1. Start at about 30% of the maximum realistic value of the claim, unless there is a reason to do otherwise. A reason to start lower might be if you're dealing with someone who is just keen to get some money and doesn't have the resources or time for a protracted dispute, or if you know they're not going to sue. A reason to start higher might be if you're two weeks from an employment tribunal and you just want to get the deal done.

2. You know your employee. What baggage are they bringing to the table? Are they bad with money? Will a quick resolution with prompt payment be attractive to them? If so, consider going in hard and fast with an attractive financial sum that is only available for acceptance for a short period. Or are they more worried about getting another job than the money? In that case, you might include some non-monetary elements in the settlement package and perhaps hold back slightly on any financial offer. Chapter 8 covers some possible elements to consider.

3. You may be able to make a lower financial offer if you show you've considered the employee's unique position. For example, you might offer to structure the payment for tax efficiency or to waive post-termination restrictions.

How long should you leave your offer open?

How long you leave an offer on the table and whether you impose a deadline for acceptance depends on the imperatives facing the business and the employee. The *Acas Code of Practice on Settlement Agreements* (Code of Practice) suggests giving the employee ten calendar days to consider the settlement agreement and receive independent advice. However, that is best practice; it is not the law (although, if you're having a pre-termination discussion, failure to comply with the Code of Practice might mean a judge deciding the conversation is not protected).

There is no benefit in imposing a deadline unless the employee is faffing around. So, if they don't reply and instead keep you waiting, then by all means say, 'This offer is only open until the end of next week'. This is unusual, though. Normally, both sides are keen to reach an agreement. Generally, you see delays only when an employee isn't serious about negotiating a settlement (in which case, definitely impose a deadline to create urgency) or if they have mental health issues (in which case, there's little you can do, and imposing a deadline might be counterproductive).

Chapter 8

Seven secret weapons: things you can give that the employee will want

It's not all about the money. Offering the right incentive to the right employee can cut the cost of the settlement package and make for a smooth negotiation. Here are ten suggestions for non-monetary incentives that will cost the business nothing (or next to nothing) but may be just as persuasive as a wad of cash.

1. Offer a reference and an agreed leaving announcement

Employees who are leaving the business on less than good terms with management are often twitchy about what information may be provided to their new employer. Of course, it's risky to give a bad reference or no reference in case your ex-employee claims discrimination or victimisation.

Equally, you cannot provide a misleading reference as this might expose the business to a claim by the new employer of negligent misstatement. Basically, you can't make the person out to be employee of the year if they are leaving because of misconduct. However, a basic factual reference (name, dates of employment, job title) is usually possible and can hold great value to the employee while costing your business nothing.

If you agree to provide a fuller reference, agree the exact text in advance and annexe this to the settlement agreement so there can be no arguments later. Add that you will not be obliged to say anything other than the agreed text and that a refusal to answer questions from prospective employers will not constitute a breach of the agreement.

You could also offer an agreed announcement about the employee's departure from the business. Again, this gives them some control over what is said about them.

2. Offer a non-disparagement clause

You could agree that the business will not make derogatory statements about the employee once they have gone. You need to be careful how you word any clause like this as it is hard to control everything your employees might say in the future. However, you could offer to 'use reasonable efforts' to ensure that, say, the business's directors do not make derogatory statements.

3. Class the employee as a good leaver

If the business is listed and the employee is involved in a share option scheme, check the scheme's rules. The business is likely to have the discretion to classify the employee as a 'bad leaver' or 'good leaver'. This can make a big difference to the value of their options. If it is within your gift to do so, designating the departing employee as a 'good leaver' can be a powerful negotiating point.

4. Help the employee with their tax bill

As shown in Chapter 4, splitting a settlement sum across two tax years may be beneficial to the employee.

5. Transfer company property to the employee

The employee might have a work laptop or work phone. You'd need to wipe all business information first, but there is often value to the employee in being able to keep such equipment. Older equipment especially is likely to be of little or no value on return to the business. It saves you having to arrange to get rid of it if nothing else!

Similarly, some people are particularly attached to their company car, and allowing them to buy it, perhaps at a discount, sometimes pushes the negotiations across the finishing line.

6. Keep the employee 'on the books' while they look for their next job

Extending employment a little (once you have an agreed and signed settlement) can be important to an employee who doesn't want a gap between jobs on their CV. This may involve the employee signing a primary settlement agreement and then a separate 're-affirmation' agreement at the termination date to settle any claims that might have arisen since the original agreement. This is a technical point, and it's best to take advice on drafting if this situation arises.

7. Provide outplacement support for securing a new job

Larger businesses often already have terms in place with providers, meaning this can be a low-cost incentive.

8. Grant continued access to employee benefits

Allow the employee to remain part of certain benefit schemes for a limited period post-termination, such as private healthcare, gym memberships or employee assistance programmes. This gesture is often inexpensive for the business, depending on the existing arrangements.

9. Extend or provide training opportunities

Offer the departing employee access to training courses, certifications, or professional development resources during their notice period or for a short time thereafter. If the company already subscribes to training platforms, the cost may be negligible.

10. Allow flexible resignation timing

Give the employee flexibility in their resignation date to align with personal plans or the start date of a new job. For example, letting them resign at the end of the next quarter might allow for a smoother transition. Just make sure you agree the money aspect of this; do they get paid (extra) for the additional time they remain in employment, and at what rate?

Chapter 9

Common employee strategies and how to respond

There are some common tactics that employees use to gain an advantage in settlement negotiations. It's important you're aware of these – forewarned is forearmed. This chapter explores a few of the most common tactics and how to deal with them.

Strategy 1: Raising grievances

To ensure they get what they want, employees may make not striking a deal painful for you. They may make every effort to make their continued presence in the workplace a problem, typically by raising grievances (and the plural is used here for good reason). They may throw mud, put you to lots of work and involve a multitude of people. They'll do this partly to bolster their position, so they can show they have claims they could bring against you. They'll sometimes also do it to be disruptive, knowing your patience will wear thin and a deal will start to look attractive.

To deal with this, you should:

- Keep your cool (hard as it is) and be super-professional. If the employee knows you're frustrated, they may see this as a sign of weakness. So, stay polite.

- Follow your processes exactly as you would have done had you not been in settlement negotiations. Schedule meetings and insist the employee attends. Insist they produce documents so you can investigate their grievances. Insist they attend occupational health appointments.
- Make sure anyone liaising with the employee about a potential settlement is, on the face of it, completely disconnected from any grievance process. If the employee starts withdrawing their grievances as a negotiation card, that person can foil them by saying, 'I know nothing about that. It's being dealt with separately'.
- Ensure that every interaction, grievance and procedural step is meticulously documented. This serves two purposes: (a) it demonstrates to the employee (and any potential tribunal) that you are handling matters fairly and professionally; and (b) it provides a clear record should litigation arise, showing that you acted consistently and in line with your policies.
- Consider, if the grievance(s) are particularly complex or voluminous, bringing in an independent investigator. This can add credibility to the process, shield internal staff from further disruption, and demonstrate to the employee and any tribunal that you are taking the issues seriously. The HR Inner Circle maintains a list of independent investigators at https://bit.ly/grievanceinvestigations.

Strategy 2: Firing off subject access requests

Subject access requests (SARs) are requests made in writing by an employee or ex-employee for personal information held about them. This can include any data in which the person is identifiable, either by name or description. The employee may hope to put you to a lot of work or uncover some bad behaviour on your part (typically an unwisely worded email or WhatsApp message between managers), which can play into their hands.

To deal with this, you should:

- Bear in mind the time frame for response. The *Data Protection Act 2018* states that you should respond within one month, but if the request is complex, you can extend that by up to two extra months. You must let the employee know if you are going to need that extra time. Thinking sensibly about this, are you really going to negotiate with the employee for a month – let alone three months? Certainly, don't ignore the request, but don't let it distract from your focus on settlement. Get someone outside of the settlement negotiation to start pulling together the documentation that is caught by the request. The same person can send letters asking the employee for more information on their request and for its scope to be narrowed. This puts the employee back to work – it's a war of attrition on these things.
- Take pre-emptive action by not writing down things you wouldn't say to the employee's face (unless the communication is with a legal adviser and covered by privilege, as covered in Chapter 6). If there's nothing

in writing, there's nothing to disclose. What you really don't want when you get a SAR is to uncover a whole bunch of damaging emails discussing how to get rid of the employee.

- Make any deal conditional on the employee withdrawing any active SARs and undertaking not to lodge further requests. It's not clear whether an undertaking in a settlement agreement not to lodge future SARs is enforceable – but it's likely that it's not. However, it's better to have it in the settlement agreement anyway because it does no harm, and the employee won't know that it might not be enforceable.

Strategy 3: Going off sick

It's not uncommon for employees to go off sick when their employment is nearing an end for disciplinary, performance or similar reasons. Sometimes, they are genuinely unwell, but sometimes it is (at least partly) tactical. This makes communication harder, and the employee may also increase the settlement amount they are asking for – by claiming that it's your treatment of them that has made them ill.

To deal with this, you should:

- Acknowledge the illness. Start by recognising the employee's stated condition. Avoid making assumptions about whether the illness is genuine, as doing so could appear insensitive or undermine your position later.

- Maintain professionalism. Keep communication calm and empathetic to avoid escalating claims of mistreatment.
- Ensure that the absence is handled in line with your company's sickness absence procedures. This includes requiring timely medical certificates and conducting return-to-work interviews if appropriate. Avoid any deviation from your policy that could give the impression of unfair treatment.
- Only pay the employee full sick pay if they are contractually entitled to it. Otherwise, pay statutory sick pay only.
- Get occupational health involved at a very early stage to understand the incapacity issue and put together a return-to-work plan. Make the employee think you want them back at work, even if it's the last thing you want!

Chapter 10
Employer strategies: how to keep the pressure on

This chapter explores seven strategies you can use to push the settlement process forward and encourage the employee to settle for a reasonable amount.

Strategy 1: Remind the employee of their duty to mitigate their losses

If the employee has already left their job, any compensation (and the sum you will base your negotiations on) is directly linked to their loss of earnings. The employee is under a duty to mitigate, which means looking for a job and keeping those losses to a minimum. If they can't prove they have made reasonable efforts to find new work, or if they unreasonably turn down a suitable job offer, it will mean a tribunal will award them less compensation.

You can keep the pressure on the ex-employee by setting up job searches yourself for suitable roles. This is a win-win. If they apply for the jobs and get one, it guillotines their loss of earnings claim.

Regularly send them links to suitable jobs, ask if they have applied and express your concern that if they haven't applied (or don't), they are failing in their duty to mitigate their losses. This will make the employee uncomfortable and aid negotiation.

This also has a secondary use because if a settlement is not reached and the matter goes to a tribunal, you will have a clear record of the job market when the employee left. You can use this as the basis of what's called a 'counter schedule of loss' – a document where you set out that the employee's claimed loss of earnings sum is unreasonable because they ignored opportunities for new employment.

Strategy 2: Sow the seed of doubt

The chances of winning at a tribunal are rarely 100%, not least because tribunal judges are human! Many lawyers say there is never more than an 80% chance of winning a contested case, no matter how good it is. So, unless there is an undeniably valid claim, you can warn the employee during the negotiations that they have no guarantee of winning. Sowing doubt in the employee's mind by highlighting the weaknesses in their case can be effective, especially if they want to move on with their life.

Strategy 3: A bird in the hand is worth two in the bush

Bringing a tribunal claim can be a stressful and drawn-out process. It will take well over a year for a more complex multi-day case like a discrimination claim to be heard. While it may sound cynical, many employees might prefer to accept some money in their hand now, and you can use this to try to persuade them to settle.

Strategy 4: Make use of the rules on reduced compensation

You now know that a tribunal will award less compensation if the claimant hasn't tried to find a new job.

However, compensation could also be reduced in the following situations:

- The employee was partly to blame for their dismissal.
- The employee would have been dismissed fairly within a short time in any event. If, for example, there is a company restructuring on the horizon, this might have led to you making the employee redundant anyway. Another example is if alleged misconduct comes to light after the employee has left that, had you known about it during employment, might have justified dismissal in any case. The legal term for this is an 'intervening event'.
- The dismissal process was unfair, but the tribunal accepts you would have dismissed the employee fairly if you had followed the right procedure. This is called the 'no difference' rule (also known as a *Polkey* reduction, after a famous case).

If you believe any of these situations apply, you can use this to bolster an argument that the employee can't claim significant loss of earnings and should accept the settlement on the table.

Strategy 5: Keep pushing open processes

This applies if the employee is still employed during the negotiations. Don't make the mistake of letting open disciplinary, consultation, performance management or other live processes slip whilst you negotiate. The threat of these processes usually helps to keep the employee at the table. It also gives the impression that you would happily remove them the old-fashioned way and that you don't need to negotiate – you have other options. For a little bit of work, this is a very powerful strategy that can bring down the size of the settlement the employee is holding out for by a considerable amount.

Strategy 6: Highlight the risk of the employee being out of pocket

Even if they win their claim, the employee will not win back any legal costs, except under exceptional circumstances. So, they may walk away with little net gain or even be significantly out of pocket if they engage lawyers. This risk increases in discrimination cases, which often last several days.

Make sure the employee is aware of all this.

Strategy 7: Assert unreasonable conduct

This strategy applies if you negotiate once proceedings have been issued. You may feel the employee is adopting an unreasonable position on settlement and your offer represents at least as much (if not more) than they would get on their best day in tribunal. In this case, consider sending this information across, alongside your 'best and final' offer, in a letter headed 'without prejudice save as to costs'.

As mentioned above, costs are very rarely awarded in the tribunal, but letters such as this can be a very powerful negotiation tool. The letter will say that if the employee does not accept the offer and goes to the tribunal and loses (or wins but receives less than the amount you have offered), you will bring the part of the letter about costs to the tribunal's attention. You will make the case to the tribunal that the employee, in continuing the claim after receiving this offer, acted unreasonably and should have to pay your costs from the date of the letter.

But be very cautious about using this strategy. Judges really don't like it, and occasionally the employee can crack the 'without prejudice' rule and use the letter to argue that it is you who is conducting the proceedings unreasonably and so you should have to pay, or contribute to, their legal costs.

If you're going to use this strategy, do not do so routinely. It's also worth getting someone else, like a lawyer, to double-check your figures and assessment of the claim's merits. They can make sure your offer is genuinely a good one, and the employee's failure to accept it can credibly amount to unreasonable conduct.

Chapter 11

Top tips from the experts: books on negotiation

There's a vast amount of literature out there that claims to tell you how to win at negotiation. This chapter summarises what some experts in the field – from FBI negotiators to Harvard professors – have to say on the topic.

Tip 1: Do your groundwork

In *Negotiation Genius*, Deepak Malhotra and Max Bazerman, both academics at Harvard Business School, use acronyms to help with any negotiation. They explain that, before diving headfirst into negotiating, you must understand your own position and do what you can to understand where the other person is coming from.

They suggest you should know your 'BATNA' – the best alternative to a negotiated agreement – at the outset. This is your escape route if the negotiation turns sour. Identifying this gives you the upper hand, so you're not left stranded.

They also say you should determine your 'RV' – your reservation value – at the outset. Your RV is the least favourable point at which you'll accept a deal (in simple terms, the most you'll pay).

Diving into the other party's mindset is equally crucial. Work out their BATNA and you'll find out how much leverage you have. Estimating their RV (the lowest you think they will accept) provides insights into their breaking point.

Once you have gone through this process, you can identify the 'ZOPA' – the zone of possible agreement. This is the range within which both parties can find their sweet spot – in other words, an acceptable deal.

Tip 2: Avoid trench warfare – it's expensive and brings very little in return

As Roger Fisher and William Ury stress in their book *Getting to Yes*, conflicts too often turn into trench warfare. Both parties take a position, defend it fiercely and only make concessions if they must. Both sides fixate on their initial positions and instead of searching for a good solution together, each wants to win or at least avoid an embarrassing defeat.

This usually results in an open battle, which costs time and energy. Even worse, both sides often take unnecessarily extreme positions because they expect to have to make concessions. In fact, this results in longer and more painful arguments.

Instead of trench warfare, try and find common ground – acknowledge areas of agreement and try to create a collaborative environment for discussing areas of disagreement.

Steven Bartlett, whom many will recognise from Dragon's Den, says something similar in his book, *The Diary of a CEO*. He says never openly disagree and try never to say 'No' or 'I disagree'. Rather, focus on what you can agree on (such as confidentiality or helping the employee find a new job) to emphasise the benefits of reaching a deal. Then turn to the more disputed issues such as the cash payment.

Tip 3: Remember you're negotiating with a human being

Roger Fisher's *Getting to Yes* tells employers to remember that they are negotiating with people. It's misguided to consider a negotiation as a factual discussion between perfectly rational individuals. Both sides always bring their personalities and emotions to the table and will often look at things – and interpret the 'facts' – differently.

Sometimes, two people will unwittingly talk about totally different things. Also, people can respond very differently to the same situation, especially if it's a stressful one. A long, intense discussion can make one person aggressive, which might irritate the other person and make them defensive. When this happens, any further discussion becomes pointless.

In every negotiation, differing perceptions and strong emotions get in the way of finding a mutually satisfactory result. So, always pause to consider the human element. Know when to back off and break the tension. Don't ignore the employee's emotional response, however irrational. Let them know you are listening and understand how difficult this whole thing is. When necessary, give them space to vent their anger and fear and address their emotions with empathy.

Tip 4: Use your communication skills

It's no secret that most conflicts and problems would never arise in the first place if there was better communication. In

Getting to Yes, Roger Fisher and William Ury argue that, often, misunderstandings and knowledge gaps are what lead to arguments, and better communication can help avoid these problems.

Even if there is an open conflict, make sure your communication is positive and solution oriented. Keep the discussion going and don't let the flow be interrupted by becoming fixated on an argument. To do this, you must first of all listen. Don't hear only what you want to hear but what the other person is really saying.

An easy tool is to rephrase what you hear: 'If I understand you correctly, you're saying…'. This shows you're listening, and the employee can immediately clarify whether you've misunderstood. Once you've understood their position, set out your own interests. Don't talk about what you consider to be their mistakes; talk about your own expectations and hopes.

The goal is always to bring the discussion to the level of facts and to keep the discussion flowing. Silence is the end of every negotiation.

Tip 5: Use mirroring

The importance of communication and, more specifically, listening is also stressed by former FBI negotiator Chris Voss in his book, *Never Split the Difference*. He argues that to understand how a person thinks and feels, you must listen actively, strategically and empathetically. Active listening makes your counterpart feel safe, so they open up about their wants and needs.

He also recommends mirroring, which is copying another person's behaviour or words. A simple example is a waiter repeating your order. Just as this conveys that the waiter 'got it,' when you repeat another person's words, they feel you 'get them.' They feel you understand them, which generates trust and encourages them to talk.

Trust is a key element in negotiation. It gives you information about how the other person thinks and feels, so you can predict how they'll act.

Tip 6: Find the 'black swan'

In *Never Split the Difference*, Chris Voss also talks about the importance of 'finding the black swan and using it to your advantage'.

Black swans were once thought to be mythical creatures – until they were discovered by Europeans during a seventeenth-century expedition. A black swan is a metaphor for the discovery of something unforeseen, surprising and presumed to be impossible. In a negotiation context, it represents the appearance of an unpredictable piece of information. Identifying and using black swans to your advantage is a critical skill that will allow you to generate breakthroughs in your negotiations.

In most negotiations, there's information about your counterpart that you know – like their name. Then there are things you don't know. These are the black swans, or unknown unknowns.

There are a couple of techniques you can use to make black swans visible. First off, ask lots of questions and be attentive to the non-verbal cues they may trigger. Second, negotiate in person. You can't get important, deep information through email because people can control how much they reveal in writing. You also get no idea of tone or body language from an email.

So, say you've discovered a black swan – now what? A piece of information isn't worth much if you don't know how to use it. Discovering a black swan gives you one essential thing: leverage.

If you possess something your counterpart wants, you have **positive leverage** – the ability to make their desire come true. By learning what they truly want, you can ask for what you want in return.

Negative leverage is closer to a threat. It involves making the other person know you can make them lose something if they don't accept your offer.

So, learn what's important to your counterpart – maybe it's their reputation or career trajectory – and use this to your advantage. Negative leverage should be used with caution. Issuing threats can result in very toxic negotiations. But it occasionally has a place when you are struggling to get a deal over the line.

Chapter 12

Putting negotiation theory into practice

It's time to put the key learning points about the art of negotiation in Chapter 11 into a practical example.

> Chris is a long-standing employee with 20 years' service. He has worked for your business in an engineering role since he left school. He is struggling to adapt to new machinery at work. You've tried to train him, but he is just too slow. You don't want to go down a performance management route with him as he is proud, and you think this will offend him. You want to offer him a settlement to leave the business.

Without going into the specifics of any offer you might want to make here, it's useful to see how some of the points from Chapter 11 could help the business reach a settlement with Chris.

What's the business's BATNA (best alternative to a negotiated agreement)?

Here, it would seem to be a formal performance management process. The business has been supportive of Chris, but he is not up to the job. The business has a potentially fair capability dismissal if Chris can't improve under a performance improvement plan. But that open process will take time – probably months.

What's the business's RV (reservation value) or maximum offer?

Chris will be entitled to notice pay in accordance with his contract (which, given his length of service, will be at least 12 weeks). He'll also get any accrued but untaken holiday and any other employment sums due to him.

Looking at unfair dismissal risk if the company were to mishandle his dismissal, he has 20 years' service and this, along with his age and weekly pay, would determine any basic award. On top of this, there would be a possible compensatory award for loss of earnings of up to one year's gross salary.

Now, the business won't want to set its RV at the top of these figures. It has another option here – an open process that carries limited risk. It shouldn't be writing a blank cheque. There are also the costs of getting a settlement agreement sorted to think about, including paying for Chris's legal costs.

However, if the company doesn't settle, Chris will stay in employment for another three months at least while it goes through a performance improvement plan – that's three months of pay which can be diverted into a compensatory offer (and paid tax free).

The business's top-line offer should take all of this into account. A figure of three to four months' salary might be reasonable.

What is Chris's BATNA?

Does Chris realise how much he's struggling at work? Is he concerned he can't get up to speed? He may feel quite vulnerable, and this is something the business can use in negotiations. In particular, it could begin an open performance management process alongside settlement discussions. However, the business needs to be mindful that Chris is proud and avoid dwelling too negatively on his current performance.

What is the ZOPA (zone of possible agreement)?

Although the monetary offer may be fairly small, the business could focus on 'softer' elements, such as a reference, training and outplacement services. Chris has never worked anywhere else, so he will need support in the job market. Perhaps acknowledging that is a good way to reach a settlement.

Is there a black swan here?

The company might discover that Chris is unhappy with his job now it involves new machinery and is ready for a new challenge. This would make the negotiations easier. Or there may be a projection suggesting that a headcount reduction will be necessary once this machinery is fully operational. This could give the business another line of argument that is not related to Chris's individual performance. We know Chris is proud – he might be more willing to entertain a negotiated redundancy-style agreement.

Chapter 13

How to create a legally binding settlement agreement

The desired outcome of your negotiation process is to have a settlement agreement signed, sealed and delivered. This is a legally binding contract used to end the employment relationship (or settle disputes) on agreed terms. Its main feature is that it waives an individual's right to make a claim to a court or employment tribunal on the matters covered in the agreement.

Formal requirements of a settlement agreement

For a settlement agreement to be legally binding and prevent an employee from being able to bring tribunal proceedings, it must meet six conditions:

1. It must be in writing.

2. It must relate to a particular complaint or set of proceedings. Simply saying that the agreement is in 'full and final settlement of all claims' will not be good enough to contract out of employment tribunal claims. The agreement must specifically state what claims it

covers – although it's a wise move to include a general waiver as well.

3. The employee must have received advice from an independent adviser. This is usually a qualified lawyer, but it can be certain certified trade union officials or a certified and authorised advice centre worker.
4. The independent adviser must have a current contract of insurance or professional indemnity insurance in place.
5. The agreement must identify the adviser.
6. The agreement must state that it satisfies the statutory conditions regulating settlement agreements.

Settlement agreements are generally drafted by solicitors, although Acas has a template at www.acas.org.uk/settlement-agreement-template.

What can you not include in the agreement?

There are some claims that a settlement agreement cannot settle. You should think whether any of these might arise when you do your risk assessment (as covered in Chapters 2 and 3). Such claims may still be capable of being settled through Acas using a COT3 agreement – guidance on which is in Chapter 14.

The main claims that you can't settle using a settlement agreement, so which must be settled through Acas, are:

- Failure to inform and consult under the *Transfer of Undertakings (Protection of Employment) Regulations 2006* (TUPE).
- Claims under the *Agency Workers Regulations 2010.*
- Claims relating to exclusivity in zero-hours contracts.
- Failure to inform and consult with appropriate representatives on collective redundancies.
- Failure to provide employee liability information in TUPE transfers.

Separately, any clause trying to prevent an employee making a protected disclosure ('blowing the whistle') will be void.

These constraints exist whether it is you or a solicitor involved in the settlement agreement.

In addition, if either you or the employee is getting advice from a solicitor, the settlement agreement cannot try to stop a victim of discrimination and harassment from:

- Reporting misconduct or an offence to the police, a regulator or relevant authorities.
- Referring matters to the tax authorities.
- Disclosing matters to their spouse, partner or close family (provided they agree to keep the information confidential).
- Consulting with therapists or medical practitioners.

Of course, you can always represent yourself and the employee might be advised by a trade union official or advice centre worker, to whom these additional constraints don't apply. Even so, most advisers will advise the employee against signing such clauses.

What claims are being settled?

There's been a raft of cases in recent years on how to draft the key provisions of a settlement agreement. If the agreement just has a general catch-all provision saying it is in 'full and final settlement of all claims', it may fall foul of *Hinton v University of East London*. This case stated that the agreement must list each 'particular complaint' to settle that complaint. However, trying to list each and every potentially relevant claim risks missing off a relevant one or the list being criticised for not being 'particular' enough (as the Employment Appeal Tribunal argued in *Bathgate v Technip*).

Most settlement agreements now try and do both – they include a general waiver while also listing all relevant claims. The latest case on this was an appeal heard by the Court of Session in Scotland in *Bathgate*. The Court of Session upheld the enforceability of a clause that listed various specific claims. The agreement also included a general waiver of 'all claims … of whatever nature (whether past, present or future)'. Both provisions were effective.

In 99% of cases, this won't be a problem. But if the settlement is particularly complex, maybe get a lawyer to draft it.

Carve-outs from settlements

With two exceptions, you should avoid letting the employee exclude aspects of their claim from the settlement.

You want certainty and closure, which will not be achieved if the employee can bring a claim subsequently. A carve-out may be acceptable in very limited circumstances, such as where some disputed discrete benefit – company shares, for example – can't be easily and quickly valued, and you prefer to settle the bulk of the other claims sooner rather than later.

It is, however, standard for a settlement agreement to say it doesn't cover:

- Personal injury claims that the employee didn't know about when they signed the agreement. This is accompanied by a warranty that they do not know of any claims. This encourages disclosure by the employee so you can be comfortable that there is no immediate claim pending. However, it preserves their right to sue you should they develop a latent workplace injury (the examples from some decades ago being asbestosis and mesothelioma).
- Accrued pension claims. If, for example, it turned out you hadn't been making the pension contributions you were meant to make, this means the employee could still sue you.

Chapter 14
Settlement agreements: practical pointers

Chapter 13 explored the key legal principles that apply to settlement agreements.

This chapter explores some additional points to think about when using such an agreement. It also looks briefly at Acas COT3 agreements, which are an alternative option.

At what point should you produce the settlement agreement?

If you're working to a particular time frame (if, for example, you need to complete the employee's exit by a certain date), it's a good idea to put the written settlement agreement on the table early on. It sets out everything you want from the process and everything you are prepared to offer. Detailed letters setting out proposed terms can only take you so far. The employee needs to take legal advice, and that advice will be on the settlement agreement itself. So, usually, the earlier you can put it on the table, the better.

When you send out a draft settlement agreement, you should head it 'without prejudice and subject to formal agreement'. The agreement itself should also contain a clause stating that it only becomes open and binding once signed by both parties and the legal adviser.

If, however, you're settling a tribunal claim and there's a while to go until the hearing, it's advisable to wait until all the headline terms are agreed before sending over a draft agreement. That way, if there is pushback, you'll just be arguing about the wording rather than the main content.

Should you contribute to the employee's legal costs?

As shown in Chapter 13, to minimise the risk of undue influence or coercion by their employer, an employee must take independent legal advice before signing a settlement agreement. The adviser then has to sign a certificate to confirm they have given advice.

There's no requirement that the employer pays for this advice, but in almost all cases, that is what happens. The employee may not be in a financial position to pay legal costs upfront. It's also slightly churlish to expect them to pay out of their own pocket, given that the settlement agreement is mainly for the employer's benefit.

Here are some key points to consider when contributing to legal costs:

1. Offer a specific 'contribution towards legal costs' in any settlement offer. Generally, this is around £300-£500 plus VAT for a straightforward agreement outside London and £500-£800 plus VAT in the London area. Don't agree to cover all legal costs, which could be pricey. It might also encourage the employee and their adviser to drag out negotiations, knowing you'll pick up the tab.

2. Make payment of the contribution conditional on the employee signing the settlement agreement and the adviser providing a signed certificate.

3. Employees are free to choose their legal adviser. But if you have negotiated with specific lawyers or firms and found them easy to deal with or agreed fixed panel rates with them, you can suggest them to the employee. You cannot compel the employee to use them, although you can refuse to contribute to the costs if they don't.

4. Think carefully before agreeing to increase a contribution towards legal costs when you're still negotiating with the employee. It might not get things resolved any quicker as it is money going into a third party's pocket rather than the employee's.

There is a myth that it's possible to get the VAT back on the legal fees if the invoice is addressed to the employee but marked as payable by your organisation. Companies have been reclaiming VAT by doing this for decades, but it is almost certainly unlawful (and VAT fraud) because the solicitor is supplying their services to the employee, not to the company. There's an old HMRC guidance note, VATSC92100, which states, 'the solicitor whose costs are to be paid should deliver a tax invoice to his own client', and, 'in no circumstances may a tax invoice be issued by the client's solicitor to the paying party who is not in law entitled to receive an input tax credit as the services have not been rendered to him'.

Be clear with the numbers

It's important you identify all the sums that will become payable on termination and list these individually in the settlement agreement. Keep taxable payments like notice and holiday pay separate from the actual settlement sum and mark them as subject to tax and National Insurance.

You don't want to bandy about a single figure that the employee will get if employment ends on agreed terms. This could result in you having to pay the employee's tax for them so they're not out of pocket. So, make clear which elements are subject to deductions.

An alternative approach: Acas COT3 agreements

Acas conciliation officers have the power to settle some specified claims that are, or could be, the subject of tribunal proceedings. Normal personal injury claims are expressly excluded from the specified claims, although you can use Acas to settle the personal injury element of a discrimination claim.

Using Acas has advantages over a settlement agreement. The employee doesn't need to take independent legal advice, which saves money. The agreements are simpler, so you can handle the issue in-house without needing to pay solicitors. Also, Acas can settle claims that a settlement agreement cannot (as listed above).

Usually, the employee will contact Acas to start early conciliation in relation to a potential tribunal claim. By this point, the 'dispute' is generally well developed, and employment may well have ended.

However, you don't have to wait this long before engaging Acas. Employers can contact Acas proactively to ask for support in reaching a settlement when they are in dispute with an employee.

A COT3 is the form used to record an agreement to settle an employment tribunal claim (or potential claim) that has been negotiated with help from an Acas conciliation officer. COT stands for 'compromise of tribunal' and it is form number 3 – hence COT3.

Unlike a settlement agreement, there are no formalities that must be observed in drawing up a COT3 agreement. It will be binding if it meets the minimum requirements for any legally binding contract and an Acas officer has been involved in conciliating the settlement. Importantly, it doesn't need to be in writing (although the Acas officer will always send a hard copy after the event). It can be agreed on the phone, and the moment the Acas officer says, 'I confirm we have a legally binding agreement', it is binding whether it has been signed or not.

Chapter 15

Ten settlement agreement clauses to protect yourself

Settlement agreements are not a one-way street. The focus is often on the package you offer to the employee. But you should also consider whether there are terms that you want in the agreement to suit you.

Here are some ideas for clauses you might want to include:

1. A non-disparagement clause. You don't want the employee to bad mouth the business once they have left. Although these clauses are difficult to enforce, they are a handy deterrent. Normally, the employee will insist it is mutual (so your business cannot disparage them either). That's normally a reasonable request, but it's better to agree the company will take 'reasonable steps' to prevent disparaging comments being made.

2. A clause restating or creating post-termination restrictions and confidentiality requirements. If the employee's contract doesn't have restrictions, or they are not very good, now is your chance to put something strong in place. You will need to offer a sum of money in return, which is taxable. So, when you're doing the maths, reserve some of your 'pot' for extra clauses like these.

3. A return of company property clause. Settlement agreements are meant to be a clean break, so you want the employee to warrant that they have returned everything belonging to the business (unless they're keeping, for example, their phone or computer as part of the settlement. Just make sure any devices are cleared of all company data first).

4. A warranty that the employee hasn't yet secured a new job. This might be important if you calculated your offer on the assumption that the employee would be out of work for a time. This clause allows you to sue to recover the overpayment if you discover the employee lied to you (although, in practice, most organisations will move on and not bother).

5. A set-off provision. If you've agreed a sum after a discussion about loss of earnings, this would state that part of the sum can be set off against earnings in a new job if the employee gets a new job within a certain time.

6. A warranty that the employee hasn't misbehaved or done something which, had you known about it, would have changed your approach to the negotiations (or potentially given you the right to dismiss them fairly).

7. A tax indemnity covering any ex-gratia payment. This is fairly standard. You will pay the employee a certain sum on the basis that you both believe it is payable tax free. If you're wrong, you will want the employee to pick up the tab for any tax due.

8. A counterpart clause allowing you, the employee and the legal adviser to sign different physical versions of the agreement which, when put together, have the effect of one fully signed whole agreement. This is for practical reasons, as it can be a nightmare arranging for a single physical copy of an agreement to be signed, especially with the prevalence of remote working.

9. A clause stating that this forms the entire agreement between the parties and supersedes any previous agreement. This is important if there has been a lot of 'back and forth' in the discussions. You don't want the employee to bring up something offered months previously and claim to be entitled to it on top of everything in the settlement agreement.

10. A clause stating that the employee agrees to keep certain information confidential. Often, these promises can be expressed mutually. It is recommended that you require the employee to keep the following confidential:

    - The facts and terms of the settlement (especially the sums paid)
    - Information about the nature of the issues to which the settlement relates
    - Sensitive information about your business
    - Sensitive information about your customers and clients
    - Sensitive information about colleagues and company officers

Example

This is a practical example of the clauses you might wish to include in a settlement agreement.

John has worked for his employer for five years. He was injured at work and, as a result, has been off sick for the past 12 months. He has taken no holiday during this time. The business has ten other employees who were injured in the same accident. They have not been offered a settlement. John's employer held without prejudice discussions with him and reached a headline agreement to end his employment and settle all claims for an ex-gratia sum of £10,000.

Given these facts, there are three things that the business and John need to include in the settlement agreement:

1. A clear confidentiality clause making sure that John keeps the facts and terms of the settlement confidential. The employer doesn't want the ten other employees in the same boat to get wind of what it has offered.

2. A carve-out for personal injury, given that John has a workplace injury. This is likely to be handled separately through the employer's insurers anyway. John will not want to settle this claim for £10,000. The employer will want John to specify what the injury is and warrant that he knows of no other injuries as of the date that he signs the settlement. This will make it harder for him to bring further personal injury allegations.

3. A clear position on notice pay and accrued holiday pay. This will be taxable and should be recorded separately from the £10,000 ex-gratia tax-free sum. The business will want a tax indemnity from John covering the £10,000.

Chapter 16
The aftermath of the negotiations

This chapter focuses on what happens if negotiation does not lead to a binding agreement. It also explores the practical aftermath of reaching an agreement – what your responsibilities are and how to deal with a breach by the employee.

What if you just cannot reach agreement?

There will come a point where you need to accept that you are not going to reach a settlement – at least not imminently. There's no point flogging a dead horse. If the employee is being unreasonable or flighty, or keeps moving the goalposts on settlement, then you need to call time on the negotiations.

This is not the end of the world. You just need a clear plan on what to do next. Remember the BATNA from Chapter 11 – the best alternative to a negotiated agreement? If the employee is still employed, your BATNA is to pursue your formal procedure (which you may well have been pursuing anyway in parallel with settlement discussions).

If you're negotiating because you want to end the employee's employment, then you end negotiations and terminate employment. You must follow any contractual procedures and a fair process if the employee has unfair dismissal rights or a potential claim like discrimination or automatic unfair dismissal. You may be able to pay the employee in lieu of notice if their contract allows.

The breakdown of negotiations at this stage does not preclude any future opportunities to reach terms with the employee. If they are bringing a claim, they need to start Acas early conciliation. This usually gives you a second bite of the cherry and you can repeat your offer through Acas.

You may also still enter into a settlement agreement at any time after the dismissal, up to and during an employment tribunal hearing. It is sometimes better to give matters a little space and allow tempers to cool. The passage of time can make the employee's feelings of injustice a little less raw.

They may also have picked themselves up and moved on with their life, leaving less time for pursuing a tribunal claim. This can make for a smoother process when you raise settlement again.

Seven tips for when you reach a settlement

If you reach a settlement with the employee, then congratulations! There are a few things you can do now to make your life a lot easier:

1. Diarise all relevant dates from the settlement agreement, especially those that require the business to do something or pay something. You don't want to get this far and then end up failing to pay on time or otherwise souring relations.

2. Make all relevant people aware of any obligation not to make disparaging statements about the employee.

As previously mentioned, it's recommended you try to restrict any non-disparagement agreement to senior employees, who are probably already aware of the settlement and its background and are easier to control.

3. Make sure any agreed reference is on file with HR and all relevant personnel are aware they need to use it (and, if you have agreed this, should not contradict it orally).

4. Make any agreed announcements about the employee's departure as per the agreement reached.

5. Make sure you have a fully signed copy or copies of the settlement agreement held safely on file. As mentioned in Chapter 15, the settlement agreement should include a clause allowing for counterpart signature. Confirm you have signed copies from each party and the legal adviser.

6. Pay the agreed contribution towards legal costs on receipt of the solicitor's invoice. The invoice will be addressed to the employee (as they received the services) but will be marked payable by the business. Remember you bear the VAT cost on this invoice; you cannot claim it back.

7. Check the employee has stuck to their side of the bargain – in particular on things like return of company property.

What if the employee breaches the settlement agreement?

How you handle any breach depends a lot on what the breach is and how the obligation was drafted in the first place. If you get wind of a possible breach but the position isn't clear, it's usually worth a 'softly, softly' approach first. Consider writing to the employee, reminding them of the obligation you believe they might have breached. You could ask them to respond and confirm they have not breached the agreement. Knowing that you're watching their every move may make them back off. It can be a helpful deterrent.

If something more obvious has happened, then you need to know your legal options.

You can claim damages if there's a breach of the agreement. This can be tricky as you need to prove financial loss flowing from the breach. There may not be any.

You're better placed if there has been a breach of a major term of the settlement agreement, as you can (arguably) discharge yourself from any further obligations under the agreement, as well as potentially claiming damages. The key part of the agreement you will want to be discharged from is the requirement to pay the settlement sum.

There is some case law support for this.

Case law

In *Collidge v Freeport plc*, the Court of Appeal upheld the High Court's decision that an employer did not have to pay a settlement sum to a former employee who it discovered had falsely warranted that he was unaware of committing any major breach of the employment contract.

The agreement said the employer's obligation to pay was 'subject to and conditional upon the terms set out below' and the warranty provisions were prefaced with the words, 'you warrant as a strict condition of this agreement'. The court did not make the whole agreement void. However, as the employee's warranty was not true, the employer was freed from its obligation to pay the settlement monies.

In *Stanley v Capital Law LLP*, the employee had falsely warranted that he had not committed any breach of his employment contract, which would have entitled the employer to summarily dismiss him. Again, the employer successfully relied on his breach of warranty to withhold payment under the settlement agreement.

Similarly, in *Camberley Group Plc v Foster and others*, Mr Foster, a former director, was found to have engaged in financial impropriety that would have justified summary dismissal. The High Court held that the former employer could reclaim the payment in lieu of notice and the ex-gratia termination payment paid to Mr Foster. These were both conditional on the warranty in the settlement agreement being true.

These cases illustrate that payment of the settlement sum needs to be made conditional on the promises the employee is making. This is an important drafting point. However, this will only help you if the issue comes to light before you have paid out the money. If you've paid it, you can't recover it as a lump sum – you can only sue for damages, and this requires you to prove financial loss.

If you have concerns about the employee's conduct and think something might come to light once they are gone, you could structure the settlement agreement so you pay the settlement sum in instalments. That way, if you discover a breach or misconduct after the agreement is signed, you can potentially withhold further instalments.

Also by
Daniel Barnett

Available on Amazon
or visit
go.danielbarnett.com/books

LBC
BC
LBC
12:48:52

Dear HR Professional,

I take my hat off to you.

Having supported the HR community for so many years, I know It's a challenging job you do, sometimes under really difficult circumstances.

The tricky HR issues you have to handle must take up a tremendous amount of your time, your energy and your brain power. I bet it can be exhausting for you to work under that level of pressure.

Being An HR Professional In Today's Business Environment Is TOUGH!

Maintaining your high standards of professionalism must be a real struggle, especially when your efforts and expertise often go unappreciated.

I'll wager you have to make decisions on challenging HR situations you've sometimes never encountered before. Even if you're part of a team, it must sometimes feel like you're working in isolation.

With so much complexity and ambiguity, do you ever find you're not clear whether you're doing the right thing when there's so much to think about?

I expect it can be draining too. You've got to make tough decisions which may be unpopular.

The pressure's on you to ensure people are treated fairly while the business complies with its legal obligations.

It's a thankless task, especially if you've got grief coming at you from all sides.

Doubt can creep in too. Even though you're an extremely competent professional, you might even begin to question yourself... What if you've got it wrong?

You've got to cope with all that, whilst constantly having to convince any doubting stakeholders you're adding value to the business.

That pressure must take its toll on you.

You wouldn't be human if it didn't cause you tension, stress or even worse!

Being the caring professional you are, I bet you often take work home with you.

If You're Not Careful The Stress WILL Creep Up On You

And I don't just mean opening your laptop on your couch when everyone else is watching Eastenders.

We all know of families and relationships that come a poor second to the pressures and challenges faced at work.

Yours too..?

But does it have to be that way?

Should you feel the responsibility of the HR world is entirely on your shoulders and that you've got to bear that burden alone?

The answer is a firm no.

It doesn't have to be like that.

There Is An Answer To Help Make Your Work & Your Life Much Easier For You

There's a place you can get all the help, support, advice and encouragement you need to ease the constant pressure you have to bear.

It's called the HR Inner Circle.

It will lift the burden you're carrying by giving you swift access to comprehensive resources and live practical guidance you can implement right away.

It's information I know will save you time, energy and effort.

It's a vibrant, active community of caring, like minded HR professionals willing to help you.

There are resources packed full of practical, actionable advice for you that's difficult to find anywhere else.

And it doesn't matter what you're working on.

Whether it be workforce engagement, attracting and keeping talent, diversity and inclusion or employee health and well being, you'll find support for all of that.

You're covered even if you're working on one of those tricky, sensitive, people problems you never see coming until they land squarely on your plate.

Timely Support To Make Your Job Easier, Can Be Rapidly Found In The HR Inner Circle

As a member of the HR Inner Circle, to get the support you want…

…just ask.

Your first port of call is the vibrant Facebook group, bursting at the seams with incredible HR professionals like you.

Just post your question and let it bubble and simmer in the collective genius of the group.

By the end of the day, you'll have at least 3-5 comments on your post, often more.

You'll get relevant, insightful and practical guidance that comes from the hard earned experience of your fellow members.

Often you'll get a response within a couple of hours. Sometimes you'll get an answer within minutes - even if it's late in the evening!

This highly active community never fails to astound me with just how willing they are to help fellow HR professionals like you.

They readily and generously share their hard earned knowledge and experience.

You Can Get Answers From Real People Quickly AND From Our Extensive Resource Library Too

> …really important for someone working on their own who needs to check things out, or just bounce a few ideas around.
>
> - Quentin Colborn
> Director, QC People Management Ltd

While you wait for a response from the Facebook group, you'll likely find answers in the resource-rich members' vault on our secure online portal as well.

It takes just 2 clicks and a quick keyword search using our Rapid Results Search Tool.

You'll instantly find precisely where your topic is covered in our extensive back catalogue of monthly magazines and audio seminars.

In under 30 seconds you can find exactly what you're after.

It's that quick and easy.

...And if you need a specific legal insight?

Then pose your question live to an expert employment lawyer in our monthly Q&A session.

It'll either be me or one of my prominent contemporaries. You'll get your answer immediately without having to pay any legal costs.

If you can't wait, you'll find where it's been answered before with a quick search of previous Q&A sessions.

Our clever index system means you can find a question, and in a single click get straight to the recorded answer.

But perhaps you need to dive deep and explore the different options open to you to solve a particularly tricky problem?

Then join one of our monthly HR Huddles. There you can run your specific situation past other HR professionals.

They'll offer their insights, share their experience and work WITH you to find a solution that works FOR you.

You'll find all of this in one convenient place - the HR Inner Circle.

It's Been A Labour Of Love Putting The HR Inner Circle Together So It Works For Professionals Like You

> It's great to see that we all experience tricky cases from time to time.
>
> - Annabelle Carey
> Managing Consultant, HR Services Partnership

I've spent years practising law and have become recognised as one of the UK's leading employment law barristers. I've even got my own radio show!

But more importantly for you, I've also developed another skill.

It's bringing useful employment expertise AND practical experience together in a way that supports busy, overworked (and sometimes stressed) HR professionals like you.

Everything you're likely to need is **literally at your fingertips**.

This will save you **time, energy** and **effort**.

Being a member also means your business and clients will see you as even MORE INFORMED about the intricacies of employment law.

They'll marvel at how well you keep up to date when you're busy working so hard for them.

You'll be seen making quicker decisions and implementing effective solutions to accelerate the growth of the organisation.

You'll make impressive time and cost savings for the business.

And those tricky, off-piste situations you've never come across before..?

Well, nothing will faze you, because you're backed up by an HR support system second to none.

But more importantly, you'll feel that pressure gently ease off.

With the relief you'll feel knowing that such great help and guidance is just a few minutes, you'll wonder how you survived without it!

That's Why I'm Inviting You To Join And Reap The Many Rewards Of Membership

WWW.HRINNERCIRCLE.CO.UK

Here's what you get when you join the HR Inner Circle:

Benefit #1- you'll get unlimited access to the hugely popular HR Inner Circle Facebook Private Group

- Tap into the vast wealth of knowledge, experience, insight and wisdom of the top 0.5% of your profession at any time, day or night.
- In less than 5 minutes you can post ANY HR question and get insightful answers and suggestions in a couple of hours or less, from some of the best in your profession.
- Fast track your impact by discovering effective shortcuts and workarounds from HR people who've been "there" and done "it".
- Expand and deepen your network of like minded individuals, secure in the knowledge they're as dedicated and as ambitious as you.

- Increase your prestige with your colleagues and stakeholders by being part of such an exclusive and prominent HR community.
- Gain confidence in your judgment and decisions by using the highly responsive community as a sounding board for your ideas.

Benefit #2 - you'll receive 11 copies of the HR Inner Circular Magazine every year

- Enjoy that satisfying "THUD" on your door mat every month when the postman delivers your very own copy of the HR Inner Circular magazine.
- Quickly discover exactly what the law says about key issues affecting HR professionals around the UK like you.
- Get concise and practical guidance on how employment law applies to the challenging situations and circumstances you deal with every day.
- Avoid the mistakes of others by applying the lessons from the in depth analysis of real life case studies.
- Benefit from a legal deep dive by the UK's leading employment law barrister into a topical employment question posed by a fellow member (perhaps you!).
- Review a summary of recent important Facebook Group discussions worthy of sharing, that you may have missed.
- Explore a range of related and relevant topics useful for your practice and your broader professional development.

> **The magazine is really informative, the Facebook group such a community, and I think exceptional value for money.**
>
> - Lis Moore
> Head of Advisory & Support Services,
> Society of Local Council Clerks

Benefit #3 - Monthly Audio Seminars

- A 60 minute legal deep dive by me into an important subject relevant to you and your practice.
- Professionally recorded content recorded exclusively for the HR Inner Circle - you'll not find this information anywhere else.
- Carefully structured content that's easy to consume, understand and apply in your work as an HR professional.
- Episodes delivered every month so you can stay current on the latest issues affecting HR professionals.
- The convenience of listening to the recording online or downloading the mp3 for later enjoyment at a time suitable to your busy schedule (perfect for any commute).

Benefit #4 - you get an exclusive invite to a live online Q&A Session every fortnight, led by an expert employment lawyer

- Gain 60 minutes of live and direct access to the sharpest legal minds from my secret little black book of contacts.
- Get answers to your knottiest employment law questions, and solutions to your trickiest HR problems, from some of the brightest employment lawyers in the UK.
- Avoid having to pay the £300-£400 it would cost you to ask a lawyer your question outside of the HR Inner Circle.
- Benefit from valuable insights from the answers given to other members.
- If you can't attend live, watch the recording when it's convenient for you.
- Quickly access the recorded answer to any question asked in the session by simply clicking the question index for that session.

- Save time by downloading the session transcription to scan-read at a time suitable for you.

Benefit #5 - join a live Monthly Huddle with other HR Professionals to solve your most challenging HR problems

- Attend your very own mini-mastermind group of highly qualified, highly regarded and experienced fellow HR professionals to "group think" through an issue you're facing right now.
- Develop bespoke solutions to the unique problems and challenges you have to deal with in a safe, supportive and confidential environment.
- Feel safe knowing these online zoom calls are NOT recorded to respect the sensitivity of issues addressed and the privacy of those involved. [NOTE - a professional transcriber attends and takes written notes. An anonymised summary is then made available to the membership]
- Recent Huddle topics included changing employee benefits, mandatory vaccination, career breaks, sickness during disciplinaries, effective worker forums and hybrid working arrangements.

Benefit #6 - access our Templates & Resources Centre

- Gain immediate access to our library of the most popular and frequently used forms, assessments, agreements, checklists, letter templates, questionnaires and reports to help the busiest HR professionals save time and get things done quicker and easier.
- Download them as Word documents, so you can edit and personalise them to fit your business needs
- New templates added every single month

Benefit #7 - build your own Employment Law Library

- We send you several brand-new books on employment law several times each year
- Acquire your own physical library of concise, easy-to-read and fully updated textbooks
- Recent titles include Hiring Staff, Managing Sickness Absence, Spotting Malingering and Resolving Grievances

Benefit #8 - free Ticket to our Annual Conference

- The perfect opportunity to extend your personal network of fellow HR professionals.
- Meet up face to face with the people who've been supporting you in the Facebook Group and HR Huddles so you can deepen those connections even further.
- Gather key insights and takeaways to help you personally and professionally from some of the best speakers on the circuit. Previous speakers have covered motivation, dealing with difficult people, goal setting and productivity, decision making and social media marketing.
- Get instant access to recordings of all previous conferences so even if you can't attend in person, you can benefit from the event in your own time.
- Includes probably the best conference lunch you'll ever have - a bold claim I know, but we use outstanding caterers.

> **"It never ceases to amaze me the amount of time and effort people put into the Facebook group, sharing their experiences, advice, and sage words of wisdom."**
>
> **- Emma Lister**
> HR Consultant, SME HR Services

Benefit #9 - your Personal Concierge will help you get the best out of your membership

- You get personal access to Nina who'll point you in the direction of exactly where to find what you need. She's supported hundreds of members over the 5 years she's been part of the team.
- Nina also works closely with the 11 back office staff that support the operation. In the extremely unlikely event she doesn't know where something is, she knows who will.

HOW MUCH DOES JOINING THE HR INNER CIRCLE COST?

There's no doubt in my mind the annual value of membership benefits is in the many thousands of pounds range.

But you're not going to pay anywhere near that.

Let me remind you of what that small monthly fee gives you every year

Access to the private Facebook Group	INCLUDED
HR Inner Circular Magazine subscription	INCLUDED
Monthly Audio Seminars	INCLUDED
Live Q&A sessions	INCLUDED
Monthly HR Huddles	INCLUDED
Templates & Resources Centre	INCLUDED
Employment Law Library	INCLUDED
Free ticket to the HR Inner Circle Annual Conference	INCLUDED
Your Personal Membership Concierge	INCLUDED

TOTAL PRICELESS

Another way of looking at your investment is this:

Because access to what you need is so quick…

Join today and that price is fixed for as long as you remain a member. You'll always pay the same, even if we increase the price to new members (which we regularly do).

…it's like having your very own part time, legally trained, assistant HR Business Partner, just waiting to provide you with all the answers you need…

WWW.HRINNERCIRCLE.CO.UK

Plus, With Membership Of The HR Inner Circle, You'll Also Get These 4 Additional Resources For FREE!

Additional Resource #1 - Handling Awkward Conversations

A video case study masterclass you can share with managers to train them to handle awkward staff disciplinary, performance and attitude problems. A huge time saver for you.

Additional Resource #2 - 6 x HR Employment Online Courses

Immediate, on demand access to six thorough, online HR courses (with more constantly added), including Employment Tribunal Compensation, Chat GPT for HR Professionals, Deconstructing TUPE, Changing Terms & Conditions, Unconscious Bias At Work and Handling Grievances.

Additional Resource #3 - Free listing on the Register of Investigators

Advertise your professional investigations service in our member's portal.

Additional Resource #4 - Significant discounts on sets of policies, contracts, and other courses.

Get member discounts on my Getting Redundancy Right and HR Policies products as well as other price reductions as new products are released.

WWW.HRINNERCIRCLE.CO.UK

> "It's a really good investment. The support you get from other Facebook group members is fantastic. Whatever your question, someone will know the answer. Access to Daniel's experience and knowledge through the podcasts and Q&A is invaluable too."
>
> - Tracy Madgwick
> HR Consultant, Crafnant HR

I'm So Confident Joining The HR Inner Circle Is The Right Decision For You, Here's My

NO LIMITS

GUARANTEE

Take action and join the HR Inner Circle **now**.

If you're not 100% satisfied with your investment, you can cancel at ANY time.

Just tell us, and your membership will end immediately. No long-term contracts. No notice periods. No fuss.

I'm comfortable doing this because I know once you join, you'll find the support, the information and the strategies so useful, you'll never want to leave.

Before you decide though, let me be very clear about membership of the HR Inner Circle.

It's only for ambitious and dedicated HR professionals who want to accelerate and increase their impact by plugging into an HR ecosystem with its finger firmly on the pulse of what's working right now in HR.

If you're just plodding along and are content with just getting by, then this is probably not for you.

But if you're drawn to benefiting from standing shoulder to shoulder with some of the giants in the HR community who will help you solve your toughest problems, then joining the HR Inner Circle is the RIGHT decision for you.

Join here now:

WWW.HRINNERCIRCLE.CO.UK

JOIN TODAY

Daniel Barnett

P.S. Remember when you join you get unrestricted access to the private Facebook group, the monthly magazine delivered direct to your door, the monthly audio seminar, regular free books, templates, checklists and resources, on-demand video courses, over 100 audio seminars and back copies of magazines, live interactive Q&A sessions with a lawyer, focused monthly huddles with other HR professionals, a free ticket to the annual conference, your personal concierge plus a bunch of additional resources…